How to Love Again
Moving from Grief to Growth

John Monbourquette

How to Love Again
Moving from Grief to Growth

NOVALIS

TWENTY-THIRD PUBLICATIONS
A Division of Bayard MYSTIC, CT 06355

© 2001 Novalis, Saint Paul University, Ottawa, Canada

Cover design: Blair Turner
Cover image: Chandler H. McKaig/Stone
Layout: Blaine Herrmann

Business Office:
Novalis
49 Front Street East, 2nd Floor
Toronto, Ontario, Canada
M5E 1B3

Phone: 1-800-387-7164 or (416) 363-3303
Fax: 1-800-204-4140 or (416) 363-9409
E-mail: novalis@interlog.com

First published in French in 1993 by Novalis. Original English translation (entitled To Love Again: Finding Meaning in Times of Grief) published in 1993.

Revised English edition published in 2001 by Novalis, Saint Paul University, Ottawa, Canada and Twenty-Third Publications
A Division of Bayard
185 Willow Street
Mystic, CT 06355
(860) 536-2611
(800) 321-0411
www.twentythirdpublications.com.

National Library of Canada Cataloguing in Publication Data

Monbourquette, Jean
       How to love again : moving from grief to growth

Rev. ed.
Translation of: Aimer, perdre, grandir.
ISBN 2-89507-180-2

       1. Suffering – Psychological aspects. 2. Separation (Psychology) 3. Loss (Psychology) 4. Love.
5. Death. I. Caron, Brigitte, 1959– II. Title.

BF789.S8M6513 2001   152.4   C2001-901418-X

ISBN (U.S.): 1-58595-165-X
A catalog record for this book is available from the Library of Congress.

Printed in Canada.

We acknowledge the financial support of the Government of Canada through the Book Publishing Industry Development Program (BPIDP) for our publishing activities.

About the author

John Monbourquette is a psychotherapist, best-selling author and Roman Catholic priest. While he has both taught high school and worked as a parish priest, his principal interest has been in the relationship between spirituality and psychology. His graduate studies in theology and psychology, and his doctoral studies in psychology at the International College of Los Angeles, have enabled him to pursue these interests both in the academic world, where he was for many years a professor in the Pastoral Institute of Saint Paul University, Ottawa, and in his own private practice as a pastoral psychologist. His special areas of interest include forgiveness, self-esteem, male violence, the dynamics of grief, and accompanying the dying.

He has given hundreds of conferences on these topics in Canada and Europe to both professional and lay audiences. He is the author (under his French name, Jean Monbourquette) of eight books in French. In addition to *How to Love Again,* four of these (*How to Forgive: A Step-by-Step Guide; How to Befriend Your Shadow: Welcoming Your Unloved Side; How to Discover Your Personal Mission;* and *Growing Through Loss: A Handbook for Grief Support Groups*) are available in English.

Acknowledgments

To the ones who confided in me, my teachers:

The following pages are the product of my own reading and personal experience. They arise from a desire to understand the personal tragedies of friends and clients who have confided in me.

I thank them for their trust and for allowing me to enter their wounded world.

Through hearing their secrets and witnessing their courage and their determination to heal and to grow, I have discovered a great deal about the mystery of suffering and about life itself.

How to Love Again is more than a mere translation of my French book entitled *Aimer, perdre et grandir* because I have added more than forty pages of new material and have reorganized the presentation of the themes of grief according to a more natural healing process.

Many people have contributed their talents to this book. I want to express a very special thanks to Brigitte Caron and Carroll Burritt for their precise and elegant translation. I know that their main inspiration for doing this work stems from their desire to help people in the midst of their suffering. This is their way of offering comfort and meaning to those who are experiencing losses in their lives.

And thank you also to all the readers of previous French and English editions who have contributed to it in a thousand different ways.

John Monbourquette

CONTENTS

Introduction 16

Chapter 1
I do not want to lose my love 19

Chapter 2
I am waiting. 31

Chapter 3
How long must I suffer? 45

Chapter 4
I go on living 69

Chapter 5
I allow myself to heal 101

Chapter 6
I am growing 131

Introduction 16

Chapter 1 – I do not want to lose my love. 19
Losing you 20
What have you lost? 21
Small losses and daily annoyances 22
Shocking losses 22
Unavoidable human losses 23
The great losses in love 23
Losing in death, losing in life 24
When you are the one who leaves 25
When you are the one who is left behind 26
Life-giving emptiness 27
Stop tormenting your heart 28
Be patient 29

Chapter 2 – I am waiting 31
The wait 32
Drifting in the void 33
The painful presence 34
Ambivalence about grief 35
Love is not always blind 36
Letting go of you 37
A hundred times, I wanted to stop my imagination 38
How long are you going to wait? 39
Preparing to say goodbye 40
Last words 41
I fear the holidays 42

Chapter 3 – How long must I suffer? 45

How much time should you spend grieving? 46

The stages of grieving 48

Joys and losses: the fabric of daily life 49

First stage: Shock 50

Second stage: Denial 51

    Forms of denial 52

    The heart that refuses to suffer 53

Third stage: Expressing emotions and feelings 54

    Depression and guilt 55

    Anger 56

    The full realization of the loss: the great lament 57

    The emotional merry-go-round 58

Fourth stage: Completing the tasks related to grieving 59

Fifth stage: Discovering the meaning of the loss 60

    Examples of people who found meaning in their tragedy . . 61

Sixth stage: Forgiveness 62

    Asking for forgiveness 62

    Granting forgiveness 63

Seventh stage: Claiming the legacy 64

Eighth stage: Celebrating the end of grief 65

Be patient with yourself 66

Chapter 4 – I go on living 69

I am drowning 70

Fear of going crazy with sadness 71

When I stopped being a couple 72

My freedom will come from what I fear most 73

You belong to the community of the suffering 74

I thought I was invincible 75

You retain your wealth of resources 76
Give yourself the right to suffer 77
I do not want to stop being the most important
    person in your life 78
No more inner peace 79
Open the dialogue with your inner child 80
Love and friendship litanies 81
The ups and downs of the healing process 82
My beloved, I could not see your flaws 83
The importance of eating well 84
The dangers of numbing yourself 84
A personal first aid kit 85
Assess your level of energy 86
Keep to your daily routine 86
Make as few major decisions as possible 87
I do not want to spend autumn alone 88
You have the right to be a child again 89
The forsaken friend 90
Do not hesitate to ask for help 91
Cultivate life around you 92
Unlikely sources of support 93
Renew your faith 94
The sight of other people's happiness hurts me 95
Is vengeance a solution? 96
The temptations of suicide 97
Contemplation 98

Chapter 5 – I allow myself to heal. . . . . IOI

Healing IO2

Accepting discomfort now to feel better soon IO3

Embrace yourself IO5

I have made progress IO6

Letting go of the last hope IO7

Caution: Do not rush your healing proces IO8

Not only you, but my dreams IO9

For you who believe in prayer . . . . IIO

My boat is drifting III

Prayer to a silent God II2

What to do with your memories II3

Classified ad II4

Give yourself the right to go through it II5

Intermittent suffering II6

You have the right to get angry II7

The dance of emotions II8

Remember that you are still fragile II9

Suffering has made you more alive I2O

I have sensitive skin I2I

When sadness has a hold on you I22

When will you love again? I23

Being true to your love I24

Give yourself permission to heal at your own pace I26

I am on the right track I26

Must you be born to death as you are to life? I27

Someone loves you I28

Chapter 6 – I am growing 131
Growing 132
Because you have loved you are not the same 133
I was carrying an unknown treasure 134
Can betrayal help you grow? 135
How to deal with holidays and special days 136
From isolation to solitude 137
Isolation is… Solitude is 138
From the desert to the inner oasis 139
Who invented the word "failure"? 140
An inner smile 141
It is time to change 142
I have seen my own sadness in your eyes 143
I am proud of myself 144
Forgiving myself 145
Forgiving the other person 146
Forgive him, forgive her 147
Trusting yourself to trust others 148
You can face the inevitable losses of your life 149
Growing a garden in foreign ground 150
Reaping what you have sown during the relationship 152
Taking possession of your legacy 153
Janet takes back what belongs to her 155
The fruits of your loss 157
After reconciling with yourself, will you be able to
    reconcile with the other person? 158
You will be filled with a new presence 159
You are gone now! 160
Saying goodbye: A mother's breakthrough 161
Congratulations! 162
Because I have known you 163

The pages of my own book

The pages that we wrote together,
I am still writing them alone,
in your absence,
in your silence,
to the rhythm of my own pain.

I continue writing my own story,
in the joy of healing,
in the need for forgiveness,
in the hope of renewal.

To you, my friend

I am writing to you who are suffering from a deep loss in your life. I hope that reading these pages will bring you comfort; I want to be with you in the solitude of your pain that may sometimes feel like despair.

I want to sustain you with testimonies and suggestions. It is said that a "good" counsellor must avoid giving too much advice. I know from experience, however, that in difficult moments, a strong and warm presence can help me out of my lethargy.

I ask that you read this book through the knowing of the heart; it must be read as it was written. The book contains a very loose linking thread that may, at times, seem repetitive. I have tried to follow the movement of the heart and its unpredictable patterns. Some of you will read it from cover to cover, others will meditate on it, many will refer back to those passages that most inspire them. *How to Love Again* has been written for people experiencing loss through separation/divorce or death; pages that concern only separation/divorce or only death are clearly indicated.

This book is intended to accompany you on your journey inward. Some pages may upset you a little; some may upset you a great deal. If so, it may be wiser to put off reading those passages when you are in a fragile state. I am thinking, for example, of those of you who feel deeply hurt and find the very idea of forgiving intolerable.

In the same way the physical body does with a physical wound, the emotional body begins a healing process the moment the emotional trauma occurs. Allow the natural wisdom of your healing system to come to your rescue. Trust it and it will tend your emotional wounds. Eventually the pain will subside, and you will then be more aware of life around you, more open to happiness, more human.

Throughout this journey that you are about to begin, I would like you to face your pain and to recognize it peacefully. This attitude will help you survive. It will facilitate your healing process and will actually help you to benefit from your own suffering.

In this way, you will move from grief to growth, and learn how to love again.

John Monbourquette

I do not want to lose my love

Losing you

Fists clenched,
I was holding on to you,
my love.

Through my fingers,
like gold dust,
you slipped away.

What have you lost?

Losing and suffering are part of the cycle of life. You cannot avoid them, and so I invite you to embrace this part of the human condition.

> *The bud opens to produce the flower.*
> *The flower wilts to produce new seeds.*
> *The seed withers to germinate.*
> *This is the continuous cycle of life and death,*
> *of darkness and light.*

Death makes no sense unless it yields new life. I would like to draw up a list of potential losses with you. Keep in mind while reading this list that every loss can be transformed into a gain, into an opportunity for personal growth.

Small losses and daily annoyances

A missed opportunity.
A toothache.
Bugs in your favourite houseplant.
A cat that does not come home one night.
A missed date.
The short-term absence of a friend.

Shocking losses

Being robbed.
Not getting an expected contract.
Being laid off without warning.
For an alcoholic, giving up the bottle.
Losing a large sum of money.
Finding out that you have a serious illness.
Completing a project and feeling the letdown.
Moving away from your nice neighbourhood.
Losing your good reputation unfairly.
Leaving a comfortable job, even for a promotion.

Unavoidable human losses

Losing your childhood illusions.

Losing your adolescent dreams.

Leaving home for the first time.

Losing friendships from childhood to adulthood.

Not living up to your potential.

Losing your youth.

Reaching menopause (men and women).

Your last child leaving home.

Losing your attractiveness.

Losing your sexual potency when you still have the desire.

Losing your passion.

Losing your teeth, your hair, your sight, your independence.

Growing old.

The great losses in love

The end of a friendship.

The end of an intimate relationship.

A separation, a divorce.

The death of someone you love.

Losing in death, losing in life

Death does not take away a loved one in the same way life does. In both cases, there is a separation, a rupture, but you do not experience them in the same manner.

Losing in death

To be separated by death means a point of no return. It is final; the person is no longer accessible.

When your spouse dies, friends and objects may remind you of him or her, but you no longer have personal contact. When loved ones are snatched by death, it is over. They become forever idealized. Only the happy moments and memories stand out, obscuring the painful moments that are inevitable in married life.

Losing in life

When you are separated from someone who is still living, it is not as final. You can still see each other, and often, you *must* see each other. In this situation, recent scars can again become wounds.

You must continue to deal with your ex-spouse. You must divide property, consult each other about your children and your various obligations to each other. A recently divorced man said he was tired of finishing business with his ex-wife. He felt as though he was trying to "cut off ties with a small, rusty knife."

Given their sense of failure surrounding a divorce, ex-spouses may end up quarrelling with each other even more, as if they were sinking in a swamp of misunderstanding.

SEPARATION/DIVORCE

When you are the one who leaves

There is a great difference between leaving somebody and being left by somebody.

If you are the one initiating the separation, you find yourself in an advantageous position. You have power, especially if you are planning to begin a new relationship.

On the other hand, the one who initiates a separation may feel guilty and dishonest. How can you leave someone you have lived with in an intimate relationship without causing more pain than you have to?

There are steps you can take to separate with fairness.

1. Speak of your intention to separate if the relationship does not improve. This avoids a sudden and vengeful departure.

2. If, in time, you see no improvement, tell your partner with conviction that you want to separate.

3. Before splitting up, do not burden your partner with blame. When a relationship breaks down, both people must take responsibility for this.

4. If possible, help your partner find resources that may cushion the blow of your departure.

5. Do not forget to go through your own grieving process before getting involved with someone else.

SEPARATION/DIVORCE

When you are the one who is left behind

If your partner has left you, especially if you did not see it coming, you will likely be more affected by the separation. You must find ways to gain control over the situation.

• Stop holding on to the other person.
• Make the decision to leave your mate, in the sense of cutting your emotional ties.
• Do all that you can to help this happen.
• Avoid playing the role of the enemy.
• Take an active part in the separation process, even though you did not want it.

Possibly you will hurt more than your spouse, but I can assure you that, if you become an actor in your own drama rather than a spectator, you will gain an unexpected maturity.

In time you may see that the one who initiated the separation felt unloved or neglected in the relationship. It is not always clear who left whom first; both parties need to recognize and take responsibility for their role in the breakdown.

Life-giving emptiness

All the love.
All the talent.
All the time.
All the attention.
All the joy.
All the tenderness.
All the suffering.
All the promises.
All the caring.
All is lost!

There is only a void.
Only death.
Only nothingness.
There is grace in recognizing the obvious.
Hard and reassuring reality.
Total surrender.
My suffering is transformed into light,
into purification,
into bursting life.
Why must I die in order to learn how to live?

Stop tormenting your heart

After you lose someone, many questions may well up within you:

"Why me?"

"Why now?"

"What have I done to deserve this?"

"Why is God testing me this way?"

And so on.

Be patient

"Be patient in the absence of answers,"
the wise person would say.
Stop harassing your heart and your spirit.
They are unable or unwilling to answer you.
They know that some of those answers
may be unbearable to you at this time.
For now, welcome these questions without trying to
find answers. Let yourself experience the questions.
One day you will find yourself living the answers.

CHAPTER 2

I am waiting

The wait

Waiting in anguish, in doubt; uncertainty is a kind of loss in itself. Life is standing still. You lose energy through wondering, speculating, expecting the worst. Uncertainty destroys your enjoyment of life.

> *"Will I pass my exam?"*
> *"Will I receive the promotion?"*
> *"Will I get this job?"*
> *"Is my financial decision sound?"*
> *"Will I be alone forever?"*
> *"Will I ever smile again?"*
> *"Can I ever trust another person?"*

Not knowing is extremely painful; some people would rather deal with a negative outcome than be made to wait. Waiting is like losing; you lose your inner peace, your serenity, your joy for living. Know that you can use this time of waiting constructively by spending time caring for yourself. Enjoy yourself; continue living and living well.

Being depressed, feeling paralyzed and frightened serves no purpose. Get back in physical and psychological shape so you can face the future.

SEPARATION/DIVORCE

Drifting in the void

I am waiting and waiting.
I am waiting for an outcome that I want, that I fear.
A thousand times I have thought of ways to hold
 on to you.
A thousand times I felt that I was losing you.
I falter.
I am no longer the master of my emotions.
I feel angry about that.

I feel too vulnerable, too dependent on your decision.
In this state of continuous doubt, I waste time thinking
and rethinking. Where is my inner guide when my
thoughts get tangled and contradictory?

SEPARATION/DIVORCE

The painful presence

When I was alone with myself,
I enjoyed my own company.
When I met you,
I felt even better.

When you are with me without being fully present,
I feel anxious.
I cannot live with only half of you.
Your presence only reminds me of what I am losing.

Ambivalence about grief

I want to be freed from my anxiety and pain, but I know that first I must deeply experience these feelings. This frightens me.

I feel that, before I am able to think of others, I must look after myself.

Though I know that I will never forget my beloved, I have the right not to think of him or her all the time.

To regain my autonomy, I must become dependent and accept the help of others.

I need to live for today in the face of pain that pulls me towards the past.

I do not want to be alone, but I am afraid of being smothered by the pity of others.

I believe that eventually I will heal and grow, but this "small death" that is my bereavement makes me tremble.

SEPARATION/DIVORCE

Love is not always blind

One day I was struck by these lines written on a poster:

"If you love him, set him free:

If he comes back it is because he has never forgotten

you.

If he does not, forget him."

I thought about this poem and came up with my own version:

"If you love someone, do not let him go

without telling him of your pain, and the difficulties

that his decision will cause in your life."

If your beloved returns, do not accept him back before making sure that, during his absence, he has resolved his inner conflicts and has grown.

If your beloved has not returned, do not wait indefinitely; bid your dreams goodbye.

Life has much more in store for you.

SEPARATION/DIVORCE

Letting go of you

In the midst of my despair,
I sometimes get a sense of immense freedom
by simply letting go of you.
I stop waiting for
a letter,
a phone call,
a card that never comes.
I stop
the speculations,
the intimate conversations
that will not take place.

Since your departure
I have more time
for myself,
for my friends,
for the books that I always wanted to read.
I have less insomnia.
I have more happiness and more joy.
Letting go of you is simple, and yet,
just the thought of it
takes my breath away!

SEPARATION/DIVORCE

A hundred times, I wanted to stop my imagination

*I am trying so desperately to control my mind
and my thoughts.
So often during the day I catch myself dreaming
that my lover comes back to me,
that my lover needs me,
that my lover misses me,
that my lover is unhappy with "the other,"
that my lover will return, asking for forgiveness,
that I will welcome my lover like "the prodigal child."*

*Then the dream vanishes and there is only the harsh
reality of my lover's absence.
So I have decided to stop wrestling with my
imagination.
From now on I will allow it total freedom.
I will be freer to write a different ending to the story,
to enjoy this fantasy,
and when sorrow overrides the fantasy
I will welcome it gently.*

SEPARATION/DIVORCE

How long are you going to wait?

When the loss of love is obvious, you can start letting go right away.

Sometimes the decision seems to be out of your hands. You may be waiting for a marriage proposal, or for your spouse to come back home, or to ask you for a divorce.

When the state of uncertainty is created by the other person, you must try to gain control over the situation, to play an active role in making the decision.

Set a time limit – two weeks, three months, a year – for how long you are willing to wait for a positive outcome. Make this deadline binding by telling the other person and informing a few close friends.

In the meantime, continue to live for yourself and to live well. If you are passive and gloomy, you will only become more depressed. Keep busy, enjoy yourself, be prepared for all possibilities. Get legal advice regarding your rights if you decide to end a legal union. Find out about job opportunities or about returning to school in case you need to become independent.

When the deadline arrives, if nothing has changed, you must act by formally announcing that the relationship is over, and by starting the grieving process, this time for good.

If you do this, you will not be tossed around by uncertainty. You will be in control of your life, even through this difficult period. As you begin to grieve, you will set out on the road to healing. And believe me, you will heal.

Preparing to say goodbye

You can make the grieving process easier by beginning to say goodbye right away.

- Tell the person you have lost how you feel, quietly or out loud.
- Share your emotions, your needs, your decisions.
- Talk about your hopes for the future.
- Grant forgiveness and ask for forgiveness.

If the other person is unable to grant forgiveness, or to accept yours, you can express it in the quiet of your heart while in the presence of this person or while thinking about him or her. You will be amazed at the liberating power of this silent dialogue. 解放力量

Last words

I know someone very important who prepared his departure thoroughly:

> *"Now I am going to the one who sent me.*
> *It is for your own good that I am going*
> *because unless I go,*
> *my Spirit will not come to you*
> *but if I go, I will send him to you.*
>
> *In a short while you will no longer see me,*
> *and then a short time later you will see me again.*
> *I tell you most solemnly, you will be weeping and*
> *wailing but your sorrow will turn to joy.*
>
> *I shall see you again and your hearts will be full of joy,*
> *and that joy no one shall take from you."*

(St. John, Chapter 16)

I fear the holidays

I fear the holidays and the anniversaries:
Mother's Day, Father's Day,
her birthday,
our wedding anniversary,
the date I knew that he was gone for good,
Christmas, New Year's Day,
all the other holidays and anniversaries.

I am afraid to awaken my sleeping sorrow.
I am afraid of the happy memories that only
make my pain stand out more.
I stay away from happy people, especially those who
want to entertain me on those days.
My soul is drifting and I feel sad.
I want to hide.

CHAPTER 3

How long must I suffer?

How much time should you spend grieving?

There is no correct answer to this question. The length of
the grieving process will depend on each person and on a host
of factors. I will list these factors as questions to help you
identify your specific situation.

- Whom have you lost? A parent, a spouse, a child, a friend...?
  (It seems to me that the loss of a child would be
  the most painful, and would require the longest grieving
  period.)
- How did the loss come about? A long illness, an accident,
  a suicide, an unexpected divorce, a betrayal, infidelity, a
  negotiated separation...?
- Was there time to prepare for the loss before it happened?
  If so, how did you prepare for it?
- How did you experience grieving in your own family?
- How would you describe your relationship with the person
  when the loss occurred? Frustrating, depressing, happy...?
- What other losses or concerns did you have at this time?
- Do you have free time to allow yourself to begin the
  grieving process?
- What support do you have to help you through these
  difficult moments? Friends, relatives, professionals, a
  community, a support group...?

Some say that no one ever really gets over grieving. However,
there is no doubt that pain diminishes with time.

In traditional societies, it is believed that this takes nine months – the duration of a pregnancy. I believe that getting over the grief caused by the loss of a loved one takes at least two years.

The amount of time devoted to grieving is very important, but what is even more crucial is how we approach the grieving process and the decisions we make during that time.

The stages of grieving

Only recently have grief counsellors started to explore the various stages of grief. Traditional civilizations have been aware of this process for a long time. These civilizations practised rituals that helped them overcome an emotional loss. In our modern societies we need to rediscover ways of dealing with the pain of grief, of healing ourselves and of growing through this experience.

Professional counsellors suggest various methods for getting over grief. As a result of my experience and my studies, there are a number of reference points that I use to help people experience grief and grow from it. Each reference point corresponds to a different stage:

• First stage: Shock
• Second stage: Denial
• Third stage: Expressing emotions and feelings
• Fourth stage: Completing the tasks related to grieving
• Fifth stage: Discovering the meaning of the loss
• Sixth stage: Forgiveness
• Seventh stage: Claiming the legacy
• Eighth stage: Celebrating the end of grief

Joys and losses: the fabric of daily life

Whether our loss is great or small, we go through the same eight stages. Only the duration and the intensity of the emotions vary. With the loss of a spouse, or someone very close, it may take two or three years before we feel whole again. On the other hand, the feeling of loss can disappear after a few minutes if the relationship is superficial.

Take, for example, a missed rendezvous with an old friend at the train station. You get there and the train is leaving. Here is a possible emotional scenario:

Shock and denial: "I can't believe I missed her!"

Emotional outburst: "I should have left work earlier."
"Why did I have to get stuck in traffic? If only the police could deal with the traffic properly."

Completing the task: "I can phone her to explain what happened, and visit her next month."

Discovering the significance: "I will learn to plan ahead so that I will be punctual."

Forgiveness: "It's not the end of the world. I can forgive myself."

First Stage: Shock

When there is a surge of power that would cause electrical wires to burn, the fuses give out to prevent damage. When the suffering is too great, the human body produces tranquillizing hormones, nervous connections fail, reality becomes blurry and emotions stagnate.

These survival mechanisms are activated in times of great distress. They allow the victim of a tragedy to go on living without falling apart, and to find resources to assist in confronting this harsh reality.

Here are the signs of a person in a state of shock:
• apparent insensitivity to a tragedy
• buzzing in the ears, to avoid hearing bad news
• blurred vision, so as not to see
• a sensation of cold, and inner paralysis
• physical heaviness upon learning of a loved one's death
• uncontrollable laughter in the face of a tragedy
• hallucinations about the return of the person who has left.

If the state of shock lasts too long, it may affect the person's vitality. It may cause emotional numbness, dulling of pleasant as well as painful emotions, and stiffening of the body. This state of shock brings on a loss of energy in addition to the loss that caused the grief.

Second Stage: Denial

A state of shock can cause, to varying degrees, a denial of reality. Your mind may play tricks on you, and you may find yourself thinking:

"It's not true."
"This is a dream."
"I just can't believe it."
"I saw him only yesterday."
"She is not gone, she'll be back."
"I have not touched his things yet;
it is as though he were still here."
"I feel her presence all the time."

The people who surround you may encourage you to deny reality:

"Why talk about it? It will only make you sad."
"Don't cry. Try to keep busy!"
"Why worry about it? There's nothing you can do."

Refusing to experience pain can be very harmful. It can cause a stifling, agitating feeling of uneasiness. The body tries to protect itself by building a shell and soon becomes accustomed to it. Awareness becomes dulled, and the armour, which is supposed to protect and save life, begins to stifle it.

How can you differentiate between the paralyzing pain of denial and the sharp pain of realizing your great loss? The pain of loss is sudden, burning and intense, but thankfully it does not last. It also makes room for other emotions, heralding the rebirth of life.

Forms of denial

Denial takes on many different forms:

- forgetting the anniversary of a death
- keeping busy in order to avoid grieving
- trying to find someone to blame
- surrounding yourself with photographs and mementos of the person you lost
- abusing medication, alcohol, drugs.

However, the most damaging form of denial is trying to imitate, or to replace, the person who is gone, to avoid grieving.

- The eldest son feels the need to take the place of the deceased father.
- A child starts imitating the behaviour of her deceased sibling.
- The son tries to become the husband after the father leaves.
- The newly divorced man remarries immediately in the hope of finding comfort and consolation.

In all these cases, trying to replace the family member who has left or died instead of going through your own grief is very harmful.

The heart that refuses to suffer

During a group session, Helena, a nun, told the group that she had just ended a relationship with a young priest whom she loved as a mother would love a son. She chose to leave him, willingly and rationally, to protect her vocation.

She talked about her love affair as if it were a trivial event, and she claimed that she was very comfortable with her decision. These last words made me uneasy. So I asked her about the pain that she must have experienced. She answered that it was all behind her. Then, the next day, she came to see me and told me about a dream that she had had the night before.

"I was sitting on my bed and my left breast was swelling out of proportion; I was holding it in my hands trying to stop it from growing. All of a sudden a large wound appeared at the base of my breast and released grey and dried tissues. Then I woke up feeling surprised and sad that dead skin was coming out of this wound."

I asked her to go back to the dream and to imagine that blood was coming out of the wound. She responded matter-of-factly that there was no blood. I encouraged her to try to imagine drops of blood coming out of the wound.

At that moment Helena's tense face began to relax, and tears started to roll down her cheeks. She nodded to let me know that she was now seeing blood coming out of the wound.

Her repressed pain was surfacing and she was willing to accept and experience it.

She was no longer afraid. She was hurting, but she was also alive.

Third Stage: Expressing Emotions and Feelings

This is an important stage in the grieving process. It allows the human psyche to free itself from the biological and psychological bonds linking it to the lost person.

This is not the final stage, as many would believe. However, it is a very dramatic one because it occurs immediately after the stages of shock and denial, when close friends and relatives begin to leave the grieving person alone. They assume that the person is now strong enough to deal with the loss on his or her own.

At this stage, you will become increasingly aware of many emotions: fear, powerlessness, sadness, guilt, anger, perhaps even a feeling of liberation. Only when you become fully aware of your loss and its implications will you have completed this stage. Many grieving people are unable to reach this stage, let alone complete it. Why is this?

Because they cannot let themselves go.

Because they do not want to feel as if they are regressing and becoming like a child again.

Because they have never learned how to feel and express certain emotions.

Because they are afraid that if they express conflicting emotions, such as love and anger, towards the loved one, they will be judged by friends and family.

Because they have a limited range of "acceptable" emotions.

Depression and guilt

Losing a loved one often attracts an insensitive, arrogant and accusing inner judge. You may be suffering and at the same time blaming yourself:

"I deserved it."

"I should have known that..."

"I was stupid to think that..."

"If I had not acted the way I did..."

This sort of dialogue causes painful feelings of depression, exhaustion and despair.

You may begin comparing yourself to others.

"This only happens to me."

"I don't deserve to be happy."

You may feel physically exhausted (another reason to blame yourself). Sometimes you may experience nervous chills throughout your body. Take this condition seriously. You should treat depression just like any other physical illness.

Anger

Like many grieving people, you may find that you tend to accuse others, which is often psychologically healthier, because it brings about momentary relief.

"Our family didn't help us enough..."

"The therapist made things worse..."

At other times, you may ask yourself many questions. (You are more interested in finding a culprit than in getting answers.)

"Why me?"

"Why did you go?"

"Why did you leave me?"

"Why did God allow this to happen to me?"

"Why, why...?"

Sometimes we curse the ones we blame for our unhappiness.

"One day he will pay for what he did!"

"I don't believe in God anymore!"

The full realization of the loss: the great lament

It is only gradually that you become aware of what you have lost.

You go through several minor "passions" (great loves and great pains) before you enter the Great Passion that leads to renewed Life.

Your relatives and friends try to cushion the blow: "It will pass." "You are getting better." "You will get over her." "You have to go on living." They try encouraging you to become rational.

Then suddenly, one day, something happens. A dramatic incident, a chance meeting, and in a flash it all becomes clear: "It is over. I have loved and now my beloved is gone forever."

Slowly, sadness overtakes your entire being, every fibre of your body and soul. You fall into the abyss that you have been avoiding for so long. You lose track of time and place. You sob uncontrollably, your body is shaken by the convulsions of sorrow. You worry that you are losing your mind.

And then, when you are not even expecting it, you see a glimmer of light at the end of the tunnel. You begin to enter a new world. You are uplifted by a feeling of liberation. You have survived the storm and have lived to see a bright and peaceful day.

The emotional merry-go-round

It would be very simple if you could follow the sequence of emotions described above. Unfortunately, emotions have a way of defying clear categories.

You will find yourself being hit with unexpected feelings such as fear, anger, guilt, shame, sadness or even liberation from the person you love.

Try to let yourself experience these feelings as much as you can. It is often easier to do so with a person you trust.

By nature, emotions are transitory and temporary. If you find that you are clinging to one in particular, it may be that an underlying emotion is not able to surface. Here are some examples:

- A lasting feeling of anger is often the result of a deeply repressed psychological wound.
- A permanent feeling of sadness may feed on an unconscious rage.
- A strong desire for isolation (compulsive independence) may be caused by a frustrated need for dependence.
- An uncontrollable fear may stem from an undercurrent of pain and rebellion.
- Feelings of guilt and shame often result from self-hatred and anger.

Let the river of your emotions run its course; it will lead you to the peaceful waters of inner tranquility.

Fourth Stage: Completing the Tasks Related to Grieving

Once you have experienced some emotional catharsis or release, it is important to move on to accomplishing tasks that will reflect the inner detachment that you have achieved.

It is time to:

• attend to unfinished business, such as writing to thank people for their support
• follow up on outstanding legal matters
• keep any promise you made at the time of the loss (if it is impossible to keep a particular promise, find another way to keep your word).

Make this new promise binding by telling someone you respect, such as a priest, a lawyer or a close relative. This ritual will help to bring a sense of completion to the relationship.

When you feel ready, remove the photographs that are around your home and put them in an album; sell or give away any of your loved one's belongings that you no longer need.

These tasks may seem unimportant, but performing them will speed up your grieving process.

Fifth Stage: Discovering the Meaning of the Loss

Psychiatrist Victor Frankl suggests that to regain your zest for life you must satisfy a very basic human need by finding meaning in what has happened to you. You can begin doing this as soon as you are off the initial emotional roller coaster and have gained some sense of perspective. You may need some help with this exercise, because the meaning may not be easy to discover at first.

Here are some questions that a friend can ask you to help you discover the meaning of your experience:

• What impact will this loss have on your life?

• How will this loss help you know yourself better?

• What new resources have you found in yourself?

• What lesson is this difficult situation teaching you?

• Which way will your life go from here?

• To what extent has your faith grown stronger?

• How do you intend to grow from this painful experience?

These questions will help you reflect on the meaning of your experience. Trust your inner wisdom to find answers. You may find them right away. You may be able to organize scattered thoughts into more precise answers. Or you may find yourself living the answers, without being aware of them.

Examples of people who found meaning in their tragedy

A divorced man: "It was only when my marriage failed that I realized how emotionally dependent on and demanding of my ex-wife I had been. Now, with the help of a psychologist, I am learning to become more autonomous."

A woman whose child died at birth: "I know now that I did not lose my child in vain. I decided to 'give him up for adoption' to my best friend, who had died regretting that she never had children. Now my child has a mother in heaven, and my friend can take care of 'her' child."

A professor, as a result of a heartbreak: "I started an association for people who feel they have experienced failure in their marriage or relationship. Before my own breakup, I would never have become involved with people this way."

A palliative caregiver: "After my fetus died I felt the need to assist people who were dying. This death in my life prepared me for my new mission. Now I help the dying be born to eternal life."

A mother who lost her 19-year-old son in an accident: "I understood the message that my son had recorded for me on my birthday before he died. It said: 'Thank you for being so forgiving.' These words inspired me to work with young adults because I felt that my role on earth was 'for giving.'"

Sixth Stage: Forgiveness

Asking for forgiveness

A major loss can reveal a lot about you. For instance, you may suddenly realize how much you truly loved the person that you lost and how poorly you expressed that love. To help you get over your feelings of guilt, you need to feel forgiven, and to forgive yourself.

But for what should you be forgiven?

• For not living up to the expectations that you created in the other person?

• For not saying "I love you" often enough?

• For taking the other person for granted?

• For not being able to save them?

• For lacking love and foresight at times?

Asking for forgiveness, even in the other person's absence, can alleviate your feelings of guilt. Once you feel forgiven you can start accepting yourself with your limitations, your faults, your shortcomings. You are then ready to embrace peace within yourself.

Granting forgiveness

Once you start experiencing the peace that comes with feeling forgiven, you will be better prepared to forgive the person who left you. Whether your loss is through a death or divorce, it is necessary to forgive in order to relieve and even eliminate the feelings of anger that the loss has caused you.

Without forgiveness it is very difficult to move on to the next stage: claiming your legacy. How could you possibly accept an emotional legacy from someone with whom you are still angry?

A relationship is never perfect, and intimate partners always have something to forgive each other for. In addition, whether your spouse died or divorced you, you may resent him or her for abandoning you with all or some of the responsibility for your children, the bills, and your feelings of aloneness and pain.

By forgiving the other person you help to eliminate the feelings of resentment that you still carry.

Seventh Stage: Claiming the Legacy

This stage is more than accepting the loss of a loved one and healing your wounds; it is even more than returning to a "normal" life. It is a way to lay claim to the very energy, love and qualities of the person that you have loved, and lost.

In any love relationship, lovers tend to create an ideal image of the beloved. It is even said that before being in love with a real person, men and women fall in love with an idealized lover. This phenomenon, made up of equal parts of fantasy and reality, accounts for the intensity of first loves. Infatuated lovers tell each other that it is as if they had always known each other.

When a loss occurs, people feel that they are losing parts of themselves. In some cases, when a couple has been together for a long time and one of them dies, the other soon follows.

If you can reach this seventh stage of healing and lay claim to the strengths and attributes of your beloved, you will enrich your own personality.

But, to inherit these qualities, you need to let go of your attachment to the other person.

(For the Ritual of Legacy, see pages 153 and 154.)

Eighth Stage: Celebrating the End of Grief

How do you know when your grieving is done? In the old days, people wore black for a period of time to show that they were in mourning. They announced the end of their mourning period by changing the colour of their clothing. Nowadays there are no such visible signs or social conventions to signal the end of the grieving period, so there is no concrete way of knowing.

In grief support groups, after the Ritual of Legacy has taken place, the leader officially declares that your grieving process is finished, in order to do away with this uncertainty.

Upon hearing this public announcement, those who have been grieving become filled with joy. They feel liberated. They experience a peace and inner harmony that washes away anguish, pain and depression. Some people even shed tears of joy.

I recommend that this celebration end with a prayer of thanksgiving, with congratulations and with a toast to new life.

Be patient with yourself

In our fast-food culture, we like to see instant results. I know that you would like to be able just to get rid of your pain. Unfortunately, it probably will not happen as fast as you would like.

The healing process must run its course. You can facilitate this process, but you cannot hurry it. Be careful not to skip any stages. The deeper your emotional wound, the longer the healing will take.

Healing will come. In fact, the healing process has already started within you. Give yourself as much time as you need, just as if you were letting a fractured limb mend itself. You deserve this time.

This human experience is important. You must live it well. Very few people take the time to become humanized by their suffering. They prefer either to harden their hearts or to try to forget. These latter options will make them very wary of loving again.

Suffering is not good in itself. Do not cultivate it for its own sake. But if you try to learn from it, you will reap enormous benefits in terms of maturity and personal growth.

CHAPTER 4

I go on living

I am drowning

Wednesday: I am becoming aware of my beloved's departure.

Thursday: I am swept away by my memories and I weep.

Friday: I am sinking into a dark depression.

Saturday: I feel like I am drowning.

Sunday: My God, I cannot come up to the surface.

Do you make house calls?

Fear of going crazy with sadness

Often people who go through difficult experiences fear that they will lose their minds. This may be something that worries you also. Sometimes you may say to yourself:

"I have a difficult time getting a handle on myself."

"I will not be able to get better."

"I feel that I will have a nervous breakdown."

"I have lost everything; I do not know where I am going."

"I will not be able to hold on."

Your fear is real, but the object of your fear, namely "going crazy," may not be. I doubt that you will go as far as losing your mind.

Your present state is very painful. You feel upset. You have lost your inner stability, and you are afraid.

You must give yourself time. Allow yourself to float without trying to resist it too much.

Already, inside you, new energy is building up, working towards a new sense of inner balance.

SEPARATION/DIVORCE

When I stopped being a couple

On the way home I stifled my desire to be with you.
I stopped thinking about the events of the day that I
wanted to share with you.
I tried to forget your playful touch.
I held inside the long conversations I wanted to have
with you.
I could no longer ask you to hold me when I had
nightmares.

I no longer felt unconditionally accepted.
I destroyed the tape recording of our shared dreams.
I tried to stop worrying about your personal problems.
I tried to stop myself from being happy for you.
I have given up my role as your protector and confidant.
I have tried to bury a past that is still alive.
A great part of me has stopped living.

My freedom will come from what I fear most

My eyes are blurry.
My body is cold and tense.
My ears are ringing.
My thoughts are muddled.
This state of unconsciousness frightens me more than
the loss of you.
How can I get over this?
I am afraid that the only way out is to welcome this
unexpected guest called pain.

You belong to the community of the suffering

The very idea of being the only one suffering among seemingly happy people is often unbearable.

But you should know that right now there are many others who, like you, feel only half alive, burdened by pain, misery and suffering.

You may find the sight of happy people unbearable. But you will also notice those who are going through upheavals and serious difficulties. You probably know someone in your immediate circle who is in pain or grieving.

What you are experiencing is important. You must focus on your suffering to transform it, as soon as possible, into a positive experience.

You are an alchemist who is transforming a mere metal into precious gold through the process of grieving.

You are not alone. Join the community of the suffering. You are supported by many people who are sharing in this common human experience, and they sympathize with you.

I thought I was invincible

I built a fortress around my heart.
I dulled my body.
I was cut off from my emotions.
At times, this power over myself was exhilarating.
I was the master of my own destiny,
master of my suffering,
master of my unhappiness.
I was a kind of inaccessible hero,
an insensitive god.
My head ruled my life.
In this unreal atmosphere, I was free.

Then one day, my ivory tower came crashing down,
my strength caved in,
my convictions were shaken.
I was overcome by vertigo.
I felt afraid.
I felt needy.
I felt small.
I cried and shivered.
Farewell nobility, farewell greatness and divinity;
I had become myself.

You retain your wealth of resources

As a result of the loss of the one you love, you may lose your confidence in your ability to overcome this trial. Do you have this sense of desperation? Has your self-esteem suffered a serious blow? Are you hearing inner voices saying that you should have seen this coming, that you should have been more careful, that you shouldn't have gotten so attached?

In these times of self-accusation, it is important to remember that you never cease being a healthy and whole person, and that you possess all the resources you need to heal and grow.

Be aware of your inner voices. Instead of saying to yourself, "I am wounded," say, "I have suffered an emotional blow and I have the ability to heal." Instead of saying, "I am a failure," say, "I have had a failure and I can recover." In spite of your loss you remain a healthy and resourceful person.

Trust yourself. Trust your inner wisdom. It will help you to come out of this experience enriched.

Give yourself the right to suffer

Being unhappy in today's society is not popular. In fact, judging by the ads on television, finding happiness should be our main goal.

We want to be happy no matter what the cost. This is why we put our elders in institutions and our sick in hospitals so we don't have to face their suffering. We ask funeral homes to make our deceased look good so we don't have to see the face of death.

We abhor suffering and fear. We are ashamed of our pain and our sadness.

Give yourself permission to mourn, to weep and to be depressed for a while, even if, as a child, your parents forbade you to cry or to be sad. If you find it hard to let yourself cry, try watching a sad movie to release your tears and your pain. Share your feelings with people who are wise, people who can accept your situation because they have been through it and know what you are experiencing, people who know they can't make it better except by listening.

This state is temporary. With support and encouragement to express yourself, you will begin to feel better.

SEPARATION/DIVORCE

I do not want to stop being the most important person in your life

I was never the best at anything.
For you, I was the most important,
the indispensable one,
the only one.

You told me that I was
the only one who understood you,
the only one who could reach you,
the only one who could console you,
the only one who could love you.

I cannot accept being just "a friend."
I cannot accept being like everyone else.
I cannot accept being just myself, without your admiration.
I want to be unique, unique in your eyes.

No more inner peace

Your loss has been great: do not minimize it!

You have been clobbered; your plans have been overturned, your inner peace has been shattered.

There is an insane dialogue going on in your head. The different voices are accusing each other, acting as if the leader of the group, or the conductor of the orchestra, has lost all control.

Some voices are accusing, others are apologizing:

"Why don't you just move on?"
"I can't live without him."
"Everyone suffers at some point — you're not the only one."
"I never thought it would happen to me."

This "multilogue" can become very tiresome and depressing. When you can, try to take charge and command all the conflicting voices to keep quiet, to give you a break and to be silent.

During this time of inner quietude, let your muscles and your nerves relax.

Open the dialogue with your inner child

You have felt how the various parts of yourself can be at odds with one another.

If you cannot talk with someone who will understand you, you can learn to console yourself. In the privacy of your room take a pillow in your arms and rock back and forth like children do.

Listen to your inner child.

Give this child a chance to speak, to feel sad, to weep.

Tell him that you understand his pain.

Remind her that you do not blame her.

Let him know that you are there for him.

Assure her that you will not accuse her.

You may have to engage in this dialogue with your inner child many times before he or she relaxes and begins to open up.

Once you have established a relationship of trust with yourself, you will develop strength and inner peace.

You will become more present to yourself and compassionate with yourself.

Love and friendship litanies

I invite you to perform an exercise that can bring immediate relief when you are dealing with an inner monologue that is repetitive and depressing. I must admit that I do not believe in gimmicks but this exercise really works for me. Try it.

First of all, remember there is no need to attack the angry or depressing voice inside you. It is more helpful to use this repetitiveness to your advantage.

To perform this exercise effectively you should first make yourself comfortable, relax and start reciting the names of people, pets, even plants and objects that love you.

Cathy loves me.
Tim loves me.
My mother loves me.
My cat loves me.
Christine loves me.
My hibiscus loves me.

Keep reciting this litany without making any judgment on the nature, the quality or the intensity of their love for you. The important thing is to know that you are loved. Add to this list and repeat it over and over. In a few minutes you will become aware of a wonderful change within yourself.

The ups and downs of the healing process

You have set out on the road to healing!

This process does not take place progressively, like this:

Healing is a winding road with many unexpected variations: sudden highs, discouraging setbacks and reassuring plateaus, like this:

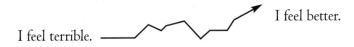

If you feel a regression, do not be discouraged. A new high is sure to follow.

Little by little you will notice that the setbacks are not as drastic or as frequent as they once were.

Already, anxiety is loosening its grip. The knot in your stomach eases. There is less tension in your neck. You can breathe more easily.

You feel better now!

My beloved, I could not see your flaws

Some days I think that I will never be happy again.
I will never love again.
I will never be at peace again.
I feel that when I lost you I lost everything.
The "soul of my soul" ceased to exist.

I forget how angry I felt with you sometimes,
how bored I was with you,
how I wanted to be somewhere else,
how I felt a prisoner of our relationship.

When I recall our conflicts,
our confrontations,
our unhappiness and our mutual frustration,
I remember that our relationship wasn't perfect.
I feel better.
And I feel like going on living.

The importance of eating well

Eating well will accelerate your healing process.

Eat balanced meals at regular intervals. This will give you another opportunity to reinforce your ability to lead a healthy life in spite of your pain.

Avoid severe diets; they often mask a desire for self-punishment.

You may want to consult a nutritionist and ask him or her to suggest a diet that will promote health and give you energy.

Although there are no miracle products or recipes, there are foods, vitamins (for example, a combination of vitamins B and C), and herb teas that have calming and comforting effects on the body. You have everything to gain from finding out how these can help you.

This grieving process, to which you are devoting generous time, is stressful enough without making it more painful through a poor diet.

The dangers of numbing yourself

There is a big difference between seeking comfort from a friend to alleviate your pain and seeking comfort from artificial substances.

Stay away from substances that prevent you from experiencing your emotions. They only foster emotional denial and delay your healing process.

Drinking alcohol, taking drugs, eating too many sweets, drinking lots of coffee or smoking too much may provide temporary relief, but they will cause harmful side effects such as loss of energy and even depression.

What about medication prescribed by a physician? It is

recommended to take medication as prescribed, but see your doctor regularly to know when you can cut back or stop taking it. It may be like a crutch that will help you go on walking for a while.

A personal first aid kit

Here are a few suggestions to help you be good to yourself during difficult times. They make hardships easier to bear.

- Take a warm bath with soothing oils.
- Go for a walk in nature.
- Have a massage.
- Take time to meditate and pray.
- Get ready for sleep by first winding down in the evening.
- Go to a movie or try out a new restaurant.
- Volunteer your time to help a friend or a community organization.
- Make an appointment with your hairdresser and be pampered for a while.
- Visit someone who is sick.
- Cook your favourite dish.
- Listen to your favourite music.
- Listen to a relaxation tape.
- Play with a child.
- Play with your pet.

These are all activities that can be very comforting, and many of them don't cost a cent. The important thing is to treat yourself with respect, to avoid punishing yourself as if you deserved what has happened to you.

Assess your level of energy

Grieving requires a lot of physical and mental energy. So when you feel tired, be generous with yourself and rest right away.

Sleep longer than usual; go to bed earlier and get up later.

Though it is temporary, grieving causes a constant stress. Since your capacity to concentrate is diminished, you should plan your activities carefully:

• Postpone important decisions.
• Avoid situations and people that require too strong an emotional commitment or that simply take too much energy.
• Take on tasks and activities that you find relaxing and restful. This is no time to initiate important changes in your life.
• If you have to deal with a stressful situation, ask for help. Avoid risky situations such as dangerous sports or fast driving.

Think about how you have overcome painful situations in the past.

Keep to your daily routine

There may be mornings when you do not feel like going to work. There may be evenings when you feel like sitting in front of a noisy television and dwelling on sombre thoughts.

Instead of surrendering to these moods, find constructive and relaxing activities. Get out of bed and start your day with music you love, with a relaxing cup of tea or coffee, or with a walk around the block. Give yourself moments of retreat during the day. Find an oasis for regrouping no matter where you are: in a park, a café, your car, even the washroom at your office!

Even though your heart is in turmoil, keep to your daily routine. Following a regular schedule will give you the feeling that you are leading a normal and structured life.

When you catch yourself having a useless argument with yourself over the simplest tasks, such as what to eat or what to wear, put a stop to it. Perform these daily tasks mechanically.

Instead of letting grief take over your entire day, set aside specific times when you can express your emotions more freely.

Make as few major decisions as possible

Do not plan to make important decisions for the time being unless it is absolutely necessary. Now is not the time to change jobs, sell your house or move to a new place if you don't have to.

If you must make such a decision, ask a wise and trusted friend or relative to help you.

If your loved one has died, you can ask him or her to assist you, saying, "What would you do if you were me?" Listen to the response in your heart.

Your loss may have affected your judgment. But it may also have given you the inner freedom to deal with your situation the way you want.

For now you have enough changes in your life. The wisest decision may be not to make any, if there is no pressing need.

I do not want to spend autumn alone

Autumn is upon me.
The cold chills me.
The trees are falling into slumber,
shedding their leaves.
The listlessness and nostalgia of
an imminent burial
arise within me.

Like the dying man
who refuses to die before
someone has cradled him,
I try not to die to my lover before
someone has said, "I love you."
I do not want to spend autumn alone.

You have the right to be a child again

You have the right to regress, to become childlike for a while. In fact, it is essential that you do so to express your emotions and thus regain your balance.

Trust that this return to childhood is only temporary. The adult in you will soon take control of your situation again.

You have the right to seek comfort and understanding from a close relative or friend. You may need a hug. Know that it is perfectly natural to ask for such a gesture of affection from people who care about you and who can give it to you spontaneously.

If you have difficulty making such requests or even reading these lines, I can understand. Making yourself dependent and vulnerable like this is threatening. Know that you can express this need while retaining full autonomy and self-control.

The forsaken friend

My friend,
I have forgotten you,
I have neglected you,
I have stopped seeing you
because the one I love is gone.

On my lonely journey,
I would like to send you a card,
an SOS, a cry.

In my heart, I am sure that you will welcome me,
in the name of our unforgotten friendship
built through our youth,
through our mutual dependence,
through aspiring to the same goal.

I need to know, to feel that you are listening to me.
Tell me.
Will you be there for me?

Do not hesitate to ask for help

Often we are ashamed of being rejected or abandoned and so we choose to isolate ourselves. We are afraid of boring people with our problems. Instead of being vulnerable we choose to wear the superhero's mask.

When we are most in need, we are afraid of letting our weak side show. We are afraid to ask for support.

Yet asking for help is the most human and courageous thing you can do. This is why people who are grieving have a support network made up of friends. It is often easier to call on friends, who have more distance and perspective, than on relatives, who may themselves be grieving the same loss.

You can also join a support group of people who are going through a similar experience.

If you wish to remain anonymous, you can call a help line.

You can arrange to visit a friend, get invited for a meal, plan activities for the weekend.

You may find that a lot of people around you have the ability to listen and to be compassionate: the convenience store owner, a neighbour, the janitor.... Be attentive and you may meet many wise angels!

Cultivate life around you

A palliative care worker once told me that her work with dying people caused her to surround herself with living things and made her more attentive to the birth of life around her.

In your own way you are also expecting a form of death in yourself. For that reason creating life around you is important. Here are some simple ways to embrace life:

- Grow a garden.
- Care for some plants.
- Make an arrangement of wildflowers.
- Walk in nature.
- Hug a tree.
- Watch the river flow.
- Smile at a child.
- Listen to the voice of your favourite singer.
- Play with a pet.

Unlikely sources of support

At daybreak my desire for life was gone.
On my breakfast table
I see my plant,
fragile being,
faithful and quiet presence.

On its leaves and delicate flowers,
I place my inner awareness
and pain.
And suddenly
I find the courage to go on.

Renew your faith

You need to find reference points within yourself.

Go back to your beliefs.

Read the books that taught you lessons, that once
   inspired you.

Repeat the prayers that you used to find consoling and
   reassuring before falling asleep.

Visit a chapel or any holy and peaceful place.

If you are a believer, be sure to ask God to help you find
   meaning in what you are experiencing.

SEPARATION/DIVORCE

The sight of other people's happiness hurts me

Some days, I find other people's happiness unbearable
I can't stand seeing happy families,
couples walking hand in hand,
friends laughing together,
lovers kissing,
people enjoying each other's company.
I feel like an orphan, cheated by life.

Your feelings are natural; they will pass. For now, be aware that this happiness that you think you see in other people may be a product of your imagination. It is impossible to know from the outside what other people are going through.

Is vengeance a solution?

It is bad enough when I see strangers who are acting happy.
It becomes intolerable when I imagine that the person who left me is happy.
Who can save me from this inner turmoil?

Your natural instinct at this time may be to retaliate, to hurt back, to try to destroy the happiness of the person who left you.

Vengeance will undoubtedly bring you immediate satisfaction, but it will be short-lived. The long-term consequences of your actions may be very painful for you. You may provoke a counterattack by your ex-partner and set you both on a course that may result in many injuries without accomplishing anything.

This vengeful streak comes from the part of you that wants to re-establish your personal dignity. However, by attacking the other person, you will not regain your dignity. In fact, you may end up hurting yourself even more deeply.

Vengeance is a winding road that leads nowhere. It is often a lame attempt to revive a dead relationship. It is a waste of time.

Once the legal matters are settled, keep your contact with the other person to a minimum. Start tending your wounds as best you can. Try to forget what the other person is doing. You will find within yourself the resources to go on.

The temptation of suicide

You may be thinking of ending it all, wanting to feel no pain, wanting to disappear. You may be contemplating suicide. Believe me, this is not the answer.

There are two parts in a suicidal person; one wants to eliminate suffering by killing life, and the other wants to live. I urge you to go on living and to take care of your pain.

There are less radical and less destructive ways of easing pain and suffering than by taking your life.

Do not turn your inner rage on yourself. Express it outwardly. Hit a pillow, scream, exercise, pound some dough or some clay.

If the desire to end your life becomes too strong, cry out for help: call a friend, phone a hospital or a help line, find a therapist.

You may think that by committing suicide you will punish the person who left you. But if you really want to triumph over your loss, show that you can become healed, vibrant and happy.

Contemplation

There is something worse than an unsatisfied desire, and that is a satisfied one.

— Arabic proverb

CHAPTER 5

I allow myself to heal

Healing

It is remembering having been loved
without feeling the pang of that lost love.

It is breathing without the tension
of suppressed sobs.

It is no longer having a lump of sadness
in the throat.

It is coming out of the long incubation
of suffering.

It is being born
to a world that is unexpectedly beautiful.

It is being alone
without feeling isolated.

Accepting discomfort now to feel better soon

The sooner you accept your emotional hurt, the faster you will learn from it and be freed from it.

I have met a number of people who have waited much too long before being freed from their pain and turning to embrace life again. Here are some examples:

John, who did not know anything about the process of grieving, suffered from a 20-year depression after the death of his mother. One evening, while watching a drama on TV, he was so moved that he began to sob. This connected him to his deeply buried pain and triggered his process of grieving. By going through this he was finally able to let his mother go. He is no longer depressed.

A woman lost her nine-year-old son during heart surgery. She was told by a psychic that her child was not dead and had already reincarnated. For years, she looked for him in all the newborn babies and children she met. All these years she neglected her family and nearly went crazy. She finally accepted the death of her child and the fact that she would see him again in his new resurrected body when she died.

I met parents who, for ten years, never talked about their child, who had died of Sudden Infant Death Syndrome (SIDS). When they were finally able to talk about the pain of that loss, they were able to accept the death of their child. They were liberated from their guilt and from mutual guilt-slinging. They could, once again, begin nurturing the love they had for one another.

The people in these true stories spent years avoiding their grief. I am sure that you do not want to wait that long to grieve and risk wasting years of your life. How long will you hide your discomfort, deny your pain and live in depression?

I assure you that you will survive this loss, and you will go on living to the fullest.

Embrace yourself

Welcome yourself with at least as much compassion as you would a sick friend.

Embrace yourself.

Accept the fact that for a while you are not as efficient as usual. You are upset and even shattered by this loss.

Like someone recovering from an illness or surgery, take it slow, avoid difficult situations, put off making important decisions, stay away from emotionally needy people.

This feeling is temporary. You will soon be back to normal.

Most of all, do not blame yourself. The past is behind you. You have done what you thought best at the time. There are no mistakes, only events that can teach you how to live more fully.

I have made progress

I think that I am getting better.
I used to think about you every minute of the day
and I used to feel sad.
Now you come to mind every ten minutes or so
and it does not hurt as much.
One day soon I will not think of you for a whole hour,
for a whole day,
for a whole week.
Yet, I know that I will never forget you.

SEPARATION/DIVORCE

Letting go of the last hope

Letting go of the last hope of getting your love back is not easy. It tugs at your heart, it haunts your soul, it feeds on the faintest hint of a possible reconciliation. But you cannot reactivate a dead volcano, make a desert bloom, revive a withered plant.

These efforts to patch up the relationship are often useless and painful. They can delay your healing process considerably.

Some say that maintaining a friendship with the one you once loved is possible. Perhaps. But three conditions must be met before this can happen: you must be over the love relationship, you must have forgiven yourself, and you must have forgiven the other person. Trying to befriend the one you have left or who has left you, immediately after the separation, is premature. In fact, it can prevent you from breaking the patterns of the love relationship.

Invest your energy in the healing process, make new friends, rediscover old friends, make new plans.

At times, you will have the urge to contact the person from whom you are separating. Welcome the urge without giving in to it. Remember your previous efforts to obtain the inaccessible. Ask a friend to help you.

A sage once observed: "Life does not repeat itself."

Caution: Do not rush your healing process

You are feeling better. You enjoy this new state. You are tempted to extend yourself in activities and gatherings that may be beyond your strength right now.

You may feel like engaging in romantic affairs. You want to rebuild your self-image. You want to prove to yourself that you are still desirable and attractive. Maybe you just want to spread a balm on your wound.

Know that you are still vulnerable, and that affairs at this point may depress you more than help you. You may also be setting yourself up for another disappointment.

Save your energy.

Attend to your daily tasks.

Be fully aware of the healing process going on within you.

The best tonic remains the respectful friendship and support of a few loyal friends.

You are still lovable and desirable. Know that you will love again. Trust in the knowledge and truth of these words.

Not only you, but my dreams

The more I let you go,
the more I peel you off like a dead skin,
the more I let the memory of you fade away,
the more I realize it is not so much you that
I am giving up,
but my dreams.

Like an architect rolling up plans,
like a set designer packing up materials,
like a merchant taking down a display,
I, too, must gather up and put away my
  dreams of love:
to live in the same house,
to work together,
to see the fruits of love ripen,
to grow old at your side.

But what will I do
with my leftover dreams
after this painful realization?

There they lie like tangled piles of film
unravelled from the reel.

For you who believe in prayer

When you lose someone you love, prayer can bring you comfort. Knowing that there is a God of love can be very consoling.

When your grieving is complete, this person can intercede with God for you. But for now, talk directly to God about how you feel. If spontaneous prayer does not come to you, recite prayers that you know. The Psalms in the Bible, for instance, can describe very well your emotional state.

True hope for the future will not take root as long as the other person is still there in your imagination.

Once you have bid the other person goodbye, hope will fill you with a new presence. I will talk more about this later on.

My boat is drifting

My boat was quietly floating on calm seas.
I was headed towards a safe and welcoming harbour.
Then suddenly the winds began to blow.
The sail started snapping frantically;
my course was altered.

Now the mast looks bare and useless.
The stays are on the verge of collapse.
The hull is inclining dangerously.
I have lost control; I nearly capsized.

I am no longer the captain of my ship.
My sighting is off.
My boat drifts rudderless, listing, without horizon.
Hopeless, I hang on to the helm.

But once I have survived my initial panic,
once I have harnessed this gale,
that same wind which tried to throw me overboard
now fills my sail and propels me towards another
peaceful harbour.

Prayer to a silent God

Sometimes, God, I get angry with you,
with the suffering that my soul feels and that
my body refuses.

Sometimes I ask you:
What do you mean by making me face this loss?
What truth do you want to teach me?
What direction do you want me to take?

I know that you want to reveal something to me.
Sometimes I get impatient with you and I feel that
you are taking too long to reveal your plan to me.

What to do with your memories

Memories keep the soul of the person you love attached to you, in a way.

At first, objects, letters and photographs can help you survive. They recall the presence of the one who is absent.

After a while, you may realize that these mementos revive in you a painful presence. The person is there without being there.

As soon as you feel strong enough, if you want to encourage your grieving process, put the photos in an album or in a drawer, and give away objects that remind you of your beloved.

To ease your separation from these things, you may want to keep one or two objects: perhaps a treasured item or some letters. These objects will help you make the transition.

Classified ad

Willing to sell or exchange for something of equal value.
The new moons and the full moons.
The Friday evenings and the Sunday afternoons.
The music we shared.
The fall scenery.
The colour of his hair.
The summer picnics.
The long talks.
The sound of his footsteps on the stairs.
The ring of his phone call in the evening.
To anyone interested, willing to let go many
other memories. Will consider any reasonable offer.
Reason: personal.

Give yourself the right to go through it

For a while yet, you may feel depressed.

Refusing to play the role of the enthusiastic and energetic person is okay.

Protecting yourself is okay.

Crying may make you feel relaxed, even purified.

Little by little you are opening up more deeply to a new world of emotions. By their very nature emotions move, change and evolve.

Try not to dwell on one particular feeling (e.g., sadness, anger, depression). Try to be still for a while and focus your attention on your inner turmoil until it has subsided.

Allow the dance of emotions to go on within you. Experience it and then let it subside. Life renews itself constantly.

Intermittent suffering

You can expect to experience emotional ups and downs for some time to come.

You may have quiet moments when you can forget by keeping busy. You may even feel that your grief is coming to an end. Then, when you least expect it, anxiety and pain will surface and the dance of sad memories will start again.

A weekend, a holiday, an anniversary, a scene, a significant place, an event or a piece of music may bring you right back to the feeling of grief. If you feel strong enough, you should try to go into this painful and dark corner of your soul and attempt to understand its source. If not, try not to be overwhelmed by it. It may be better for now to avoid those painful feelings by finding a healthy distraction.

You have the right to get angry

During this period of grief, you have the right to let your anger rise and express itself, in spite of all the social taboos that may try to force you to repress it. Know that this feeling of anger is different from hatred or resentment. Anger, once expressed, will disappear. Resentment, if cultivated, will keep emerging and gnawing at your heart.

Let your anger rise. Tell your lost love that you are angry with her or him for leaving you, for abandoning you, for making you take over the responsibilities that you used to share, for forcing you to mature too rapidly.

Feel free to be angry with social conventions, fate, God, those who hinder your grieving process, those who abandon you.

Be grateful that you can feel and express this anger. Some people who experience tragedies repress their anger and turn it on themselves. They end up feeling guilty and depressed to the point of developing physical and psychological ailments.

To remain sane, you must accept your feelings of anger and find healthy outlets for it, such as exercising, beating a pillow or a mattress, screaming in your car or in the woods, and so on.

The dance of emotions

Black depression is swirling around my soul.
Yellow fear is stomping its heavy feet.
Red anger restrains my movements, growling.
Greenish love tiptoes around.

Blue sorrow is worried about disrupting this round,
if it breaks out.
Like shadows, my emotions appear and disappear
against a grey backdrop.

Remember that you are still fragile

Some days you may feel drained and unmotivated. Be sure not to burden yourself with "shoulds" and "should nots." Remember that you are still vulnerable.

There is no need to try to play the hero, to make important decisions or to get involved in pointless romantic affairs while you feel this way.

Take care of your health: get lots of rest, eat well and exercise.

Avoid pushy salespeople, needy people and stressful situations.

Fight the tendency to be idle by doing simple exercises (walking, biking, swimming...).

Do not forget your wise and faithful friend Mother Nature. Give yourself time to commune with fresh air, water, trees and skies.

Suffering has made you more alive

*Suffering has forced you out of your complacency,
out of your inner comfort.
You were stuffed, satiated, full of torpor.
Your loss has caused you to have a rude awakening.
Your present neediness helps you appreciate the small
joys of life.*

*You may have noticed how easy it is to find pleasure
with things and people that you never really notice before:*

*the colour of the leaves,
a greeting from the letter carrier,
a simple handshake,
a colleague's smile,
the sound of certain footsteps,
the intensity of a child's game,
ice glistening in the sun,
clouds drifting across a blue sky,
a summer rainfall,
spontaneous prayers,
love songs with their happy, and sad, endings.*

*Suffering can sharpen your senses,
open your heart,
help you see life in a new light.*

"Blessed are the pure in heart, for they will see God."

(St. Mark 5:8)

I have sensitive skin

Because of the void caused by your absence,
I have been afraid I will be unable to love again,
to share myself again,
to trust again.

My scars are still fresh.
I am afraid to touch them.
The skin is still so thin.
I am suspicious.

I want to be consoled
but I do not want to be approached.
I want to be understood
but I do not want to reveal myself.

I am not ready to trust.
I want to give,
but I am afraid of being rejected
if I take the first step.
My friends, please understand me!

When sadness has a hold on you

You are probably familiar with our society's myth that sadness, distress and destruction are proof that your love is real.

In this view, dying of sorrow because of the loss of love, or of the beloved, would demonstrate a deep attachment, whereas to go on living and be happy would show that the love was superficial, even hypocritical.

Such a belief is unfounded. Someone who develops a devotion to sadness is more influenced by social pressures than by his or her inner life.

Be wary of using self-pity to elicit the compassion of others. Asking openly for their sympathy and friendship is easier, and certainly more effective.

There is a certain beauty in sorrow as long as it is short-lived and life-giving.

When will you love again?

Just a short while ago you were declaring that you would never love again. You were giving up on love; perhaps you believed that God had created it to torture human hearts.

However, if you are still reading this book, you are probably willing to go through the grieving process, to heal and to live fully again. You may still be hesitant to believe in love. This hesitation comes less from the fear of love than from the fear of suffering.

The day will come when you have regained your self-confidence and your trust in life. Then you may meet someone worthy, and you will know how you will love again.

You will then accept being in love, while knowing that you will also suffer because of love in one way or another.

DEATH

Being true to your love

As we know now, being faithful to your love does not mean dying or destroying yourself.

If you really want to be true to someone you have loved, and keep the person's memory alive, put yourself in their presence mentally and ask what they expect of you. Listen for a response:

"

_____

_____

_____

                                                        "

_____

This inner dialogue will give you clear directions for your life.

Your beloved will tell you to honour the love you shared by living fully, growing and loving again.

You carry within you always the wisdom and the legacy of a deep emotional bond between you and your beloved.

Give yourself permission to heal at your own pace

You will find that very few people around you can tolerate your suffering. They will want you to feel better, to forget, to accept, to distract yourself.

They will try to prevent you from hurting. Yet, you must understand that you have every right to go through this painful experience.

Consequently you should avoid hiding your feelings behind a composed front, a pretend smile, a false attitude.

Avoid mixing with people who have denied their own pain, or who display the physical and mental signs of repressed grief, such as stiffness, rigidity, depression, fatigue, psychosomatic pain or illness.

Regardless of the theories on the stages and the length of the grieving process, remember that your experience is unique. Performance and speed are not to be judged. You have the right to deal with your grief in your own way and at your own pace.

I am on the right track

I spend less time on inner questioning.
I feel less vulnerable.
I am able to enjoy beautiful scenery.

My thoughts are clearer.
My judgment is more acute.
My feelings are more stable.

I get satisfaction from my work.
I see life in a whole new way.
*I recognize expressions on people's faces that I could
not see before.*

I take pleasure in the small joys of daily life.
I feel like sharing my new-found enthusiasm.
I sense a new life sprouting within me.

Must you be born to death as you are to life?

In the Ingmar Bergman film *Cries and Whispers,* an old woman in agony prolongs her dying. She wants to be loved before she embraces her fate. Her two sisters are unable to give her the comfort she needs.

She cannot die before love gives meaning to her death. Then a young maid, a peasant, takes her in her arms and places her head on the old woman's naked breasts. This expression of love and compassion allows the dying woman to move on to the next life.

All of you who have lost someone without first receiving a message of love may need to seek a sign of affection that will help you surrender to your emotions.

To all of you who may feel that way, I extend a gesture of friendship that will allow you to deal with your grief and be born to new life.

Someone loves you

*To the man or the woman who has lost a spouse
without exchanging a message of love.
To the couple that is torn apart by quarrelling.
To the parent who has lost a child in an accident.*

*To the person forced to retire.
To the woman whose dreams of motherhood are disappearing.
To the middle-aged man who is realizing that he
abandoned his adolescent dreams.*

*To the married couple that has recently separated.
To the unemployed worker.
To the child who is moved from one foster home to another.*

*To those of you who have lost a loved one without
saying goodbye.
To the abandoned lover.
To the youth leaving home for the first time.
To the single mother separated from her child.
To the aging woman whose strength is abandoning her.
To the child going off to school for the first time.*

To you who are right now grieving your own private sorrow.

*If the person you lost was unable to tell you their appreciation
I will tell you: "You are great, you have loved and you have
fulfilled your commitment to the best of your ability,
you are important."*

I love you.

CHAPTER 6

I am growing

Growing

Being attached to you
has revealed to me my selfishness
and my selflessness,
has brought me in touch with my tenderness
and my harshness,
has helped me discover my sensuality
and my spirituality,
has helped me recognize the child within
and the adult in me.

Becoming detached from you
has allowed me to get in touch with my sadness
and my joy,
has taken me to the depth of despair
and freedom,
has helped me find myself dependent
and courageous,
has revealed to me my fear of death
and my inner resources.

When all is said and done, while I may have some
regrets about how things happened,
I don't regret the experience of loving and
losing my love.

Because you have loved you are not the same

You are not the same person you were before this experience.
Love and suffering have opened gateways to new worlds.

You are more sensitive and less afraid of pain.
You are more committed but less dependent.
You have learned to invest yourself
without losing yourself.

You are more self-assured.
You are ready to love again.

I was carrying an unknown treasure

With shame, I dragged around my sack of sorrow.
I sought relief and comfort from everyone around me.
They all avoided the miserable beggar that I had
* become.*
(There are happy beggars who attract people.)

Then I met an angel on my journey who taught me
* to open my bag and to look through it very carefully.*
I discovered, in the folds of my sack, my desire for the
* Divine.*
I began to glimpse the abundance of my inner wealth.
Now, with joy, I swing my sack of dreams.

Can betrayal help you grow?

I am not sure I should have asked you this question. But I have. If the person you love has not met your expectations, if your loved one has abandoned you, you may feel let down, offended, betrayed. Something is broken within you, cut off between you and your beloved. It may take a while before you understand how these feelings of betrayal help you to grow.

Like the baby bird with feeble wings, you felt tossed out of the nest by the very person you trusted the most. In time you will come to appreciate the lessons this experience has taught you.

Just as the ropes that hold down a hot air balloon must be untied for it to rise, abandonment may urge you abruptly onward to self-fulfillment.

How to deal with holidays and special days

A friend who accompanies families through their grieving process recommends that they always prepare themselves for an upcoming holiday or anniversary. He suggests that the family gather for a grieving session shortly beforehand.

The members of the family may look at photographs, recall memorable events, exchange thoughts, allow themselves to mourn and to be consoled. After this session, they are able to celebrate the event joyfully, without guilt.

Even for those of you who are further along in your grieving, anniversaries, birthdays and other memorable events may cause you sadness for a few hours, or a day. Embrace this partial relapse into grief and experience it fully. You will then be able to celebrate the event more intensely.

From isolation to solitude

Will the pain of loss lead you to isolation, which is unhealthy, or to solitude, which is healthy?

If you have a tendency to close yourself off, ask yourself whether you are becoming comfortable with solitude or simply isolating yourself.

Isolation can resemble solitude, but there is a great difference between these two inner attitudes. You may be experiencing both at the same time, or in turn.

Here are some pointers to help you determine whether you are experiencing barren isolation or life-giving solitude.

Isolation is...

- the fear of being with others and the fear of being alone

- a defense system against intrusion

- inner turmoil and confusion

- a distressed outlook

- a closing to the outer world

- a continuous and useless series of speculations

- the denial of your own vulnerability caused by fear of rejection

- a time of inner and outer unrest

Solitude is...

- a voluntary withdrawal from others to be alone with yourself

- an inner contemplation helping you to be more open to yourself and to others

- an open and peaceful time of reflecting on yourself

- a peaceful outlook

- an opening to others through intimacy with yourself

- a silence filled with the love of those around you

- the profound acceptance of your own interdependence and your own autonomy

- a time of peace and of harmonizing your inner world

From the desert to the inner oasis

You may have to experience isolation before you reach a comfortable and life-giving state of solitude. Each one of us reacts differently to the idea of being alone. Some of us collapse and regress; others will rebel against any form of dependence.

As a child you may have felt afraid of being abandoned or rejected. Consequently, you may feel that loneliness is a terrible threat. If so, your initial reaction will be to deny your reality or to distract yourself with television, music, love affairs, alcohol, drugs, and the like. Find a guide or a counsellor who can help you understand solitude as something good and life-giving.

On this journey to inner discovery, you will learn to go from isolation to solitude, from loneliness to aloneness. It will be as though you were finding a cure in the disease itself, or discovering that you have to push the hook deeper into the flesh to remove it.

Stay with yourself.

Discover all of your parts.

Plunge all the way into your inner spacing.

Armed with courage, you will walk through the ruins of your own suffering, through the dark and damp caves of your inner world. You will pass through many chambers and your faith will lead you to the heart of your essence wherein lies a precious jewel. Then you will know who you are and what you are called to do.

"I am never alone with my solitude."

– Georges Moustaki

Who invented the word "failure"?

Life is not a game or a sport. It does not end with a loss, and never results in failure.

But like a fighter who has been dealt a blow, you must pick yourself up to avoid being hit again.

You will come out a winner if you learn from this experience. Take stock of the lessons you have learned:

- You know yourself better.
- You understand the suffering of others better.
- You are freer.
- You have opened up your horizons.
- You know that you are not perfect.
- You allow others to be imperfect.
- You are on the road to healing.
- You are like a scientist who makes a ground-breaking discovery with a wrong formula.
- You are like a painter who creates a masterpiece from a stain on the canvas.
- You are like a musician who writes a symphony from a faulty chord.

There are no mistakes or failures; life always rises from death.

An inner smile

Within me a smile is rising,
vibrating,
expanding,
in the silence of my heart.

It lightens my being,
and brightens my life.

Because I have loved,
I want to love again.

It is time to change

Now that you feel better,
that you can concentrate again,
that the future is open to you,
that the past is a memory,
it is time to change.

You are no longer contained by your old relationship.
Make all the necessary adjustments in your life.
You have more time to meet your own needs.
Develop new interests.
Change your style of dress.

Try something new, something exhilarating.
Travel to new places.
Go back to school.
Make new friends.
Join a new club.
Remodel your home.
Learn something you have always wanted to know, or master a skill
you had begun to develop.

SEPARATION/DIVORCE

I have seen my own sadness in your eyes

My heart was ripe with bitterness,
my gaping wound filled with venomous thoughts.
I could scarcely contain my wrath.

To forgive, to try to forget was like betraying myself.
I needed vengeance, retribution, or else I would feel
forever humiliated.
To meet the person who hurt me seemed like sheer folly.

But when I finally mustered the courage to look upon her
face, her expression moved me to the core of my being.
In her eyes, I recognized my own sadness,
my depression, a hint of tenderness.

Since that moment, that vision haunts me.
All those feelings were shared by both of us.
My heart was touched, it softened and opened up.
All the harshness vanished.
Compassion had its way.

SEPARATION/DIVORCE

I am proud of myself

When my hurt was still fresh,
I wanted to make you feel guilty,
like a child who, when he is hurt, hits a smaller child.

I wanted you to be overwhelmed by remorse at the
thought of the pain that you inflicted on me.
I wanted to place you on the stand,
to let the entire world know about your betrayal.
I wanted to punish you, to take my revenge.
I wanted to come out triumphant, remorseless.

I am proud of myself for having avoided this
treacherous road.
Many times I have felt anger, but I have not given
into it by punishing you.
Though I felt like avenging myself, I understood how
useless it would be.

I am proud of myself for having embraced my hurt.
I tended to it with all the care I could muster.
I have chosen to protect what I have loved.
Through it all, I have grown.

Forgiving myself

I want to forgive myself for having been
fragile,
careless,
wrong,
vulnerable in love,
unsuspecting,
hurt,
a dreamer,
frustrated and lonely,
willing to love again.

In short,
I want to forgive myself
for being human.

Forgiving the other person

Granting forgiveness is a royal gesture.
As soon as you feel strong enough,
forgive the person you have lost.

Forgiving does not mean
forgetting the offense or the loss,
making excuses for the other person,
denying your emotions or your feelings,
reconciling yourself with the other person.

Forgiving means
freeing yourself from vengeance and resentment,
recognizing the joy of being forgiven by others,
asking for the strength to love beyond this wounded love,
relieving the other person of the debt.

If you can forgive, you will become a queen, a king.

Forgive him, forgive her

Forgive him, forgive her
for leaving,
for leaving so soon,
for leaving without saying goodbye,
for leaving without preparing you,
for leaving without fulfilling all the promises,
for leaving with a piece of yourself,
for leaving with your world of dreams and aspirations.

Trusting yourself to trust others

This loss of your beloved shattered your self-confidence and your trust in others.

Initially you felt that you had to prove to yourself that you were lovable and capable of loving again.

Now you know that you are lovable. You have only to welcome those people that Providence will place on your path.

Go out, meet people.

Rediscover your neighbours, your colleagues.

Join a group, a community of friends.

Invite people for coffee.

Share information and services.

Listen to people; they love talking about themselves.

You can face the inevitable losses of your life

You are now master of a new skill – the art of letting go of people, activities and things that come into and go out of your life.

There are people who carry around the sorrows of all their unresolved losses; they are like cluttered trunks. They never let go of their mother, their father, their first teddy bear, their cat, their childhood, their childhood friends, and so on.

By fully experiencing the grief of this loss of your beloved, all at once, you have gotten rid of everything that was dead inside you.

The next time you are faced with the loss of someone important, you will still experience shock, pain and turmoil, but you will know your way on the road to healing.

You have succeeded this time around and you will succeed again.

By learning how to live after death, little by little you are learning how to die after life. The inevitability of your own death will no longer be as frightening.

By overcoming small "deaths" you will discover different perspectives on living.

Growing a garden in foreign ground

Like a seed thrown in the spring wind,
my love and my hope are carried by the breath of your
presence.

Like a bountiful Mother Nature, carefree, drunk with joy,
I am planting my garden in foreign ground.
With every thrust of germination, with each sprout,
I am realizing the richness of my treasure.

In these moments of joy, ecstasy and discovery,
I bask in this abundance of life.
I marvel, I rejoice, I aspire to be the proud new owner,
the undisputed landlord of these grounds.

Who would have guessed that I had sown my dreams
on someone else's property?

Then one day my host brings me back to reality.
I have become the usurper in an occupied territory.
I am asked to leave this rich soil.

My fruits and flowers are growing on foreign ground.
I want to leave without turning back.
I want to hide my pain behind a mask, hardened by pride.
I want to forget all my days of cultivating and uproot
the fruit of my labour like an unwanted growth.

Then, with the humility of a king turned beggar,
I begin picking, plucking, reaping and gathering my
inner harvest.
I must dig, cut and even pull out the roots to take
everything.
I refuse to leave anything to my spiteful host.

Reaping what you have sown during the relationship

You are beginning to feel less and less of the pain of your loss. You can go for long periods without even thinking about it.

The time has come for you to reap the fruits of your relationship.

Take up new interests.

Learn a new sport.

Develop a new skill.

Try a new approach to life.

Discover a new you.

Make a list of the qualities that you liked in the person you lost. Note that you also possess these qualities within yourself. Now the qualities — such as kindness, assertiveness, love of music, of literature, self-care, social values — belong to you.

Do not let your beloved go without claiming your legacy. It is up to you to develop in yourself what you loved, sought and admired in the other person.

Taking possession of your legacy

I want to introduce you to a wonderful ritual that will help you reclaim what you have lost. I suggest that you perform this exercise in the company of a few close friends. This will help you bring the process to completion. If you do it alone, you may experience reservations and hesitations, and give up halfway. I assure you that the act of claiming your legacy will bring about a profound and liberating transformation within yourself.

Ask one of your friends to guide you through the following steps.

1. Imagine that the person you lost is sitting in front of you (use an empty chair to symbolize the person).

2. Describe what you admired in the person: qualities, strengths, attributes.

3. Represent each one of these by a drawing or an object and place them on the chair in front of you.

4. Out loud, say the following: "I take back (name a quality) that I loaned you, as well as all the maturity and growth that your personality added to it." You are now harvesting the fruits of your love. (See the poem "Growing a garden in foreign ground," on pages 150-151.)

5. Stand up, take the drawing or the symbol and place it on your heart. Allow yourself to feel physically touched by this newly discovered quality. The incubation period may last for up to about 20 minutes. During this period, your friend can help you try out this new quality, feel it deeply and act it out in different contexts.

6. Do the same thing for each quality.

7. When you are finished, find a symbol that best describes your lover's personality and place the drawings and objects around that symbol to form a complete picture.

8. Your guide proclaims to the group that you have completed your process of grieving.

You will be amazed at the transformation that will take place within you during the next few days.

Janet takes back what belongs to her

Janet is a single secretary who fell head over heels in love with her boss, Jim. He is married with three children. Their initial friendship soon turned into an intense love affair.

When Janet came to see me, she was devastated by this impossible situation. She was increasingly depressed. Her mental health was affected and she felt terribly guilty about Jim's wife.

After hesitating for weeks, she decided to end the relationship. I helped her to prepare to meet with Jim and formally end the relationship. After she had done this, Janet came back to see me. She was weeping and overwhelmed by sadness. I supported her during her time of grief. After a period of about nine months, I suggested that, when she felt ready, she should think of claiming her legacy.

Two weeks later, Janet arrived at my office, still hurting, but feeling more peaceful. She felt ready for the ritual of claiming her legacy. She sat in front of an empty chair and tried to imagine that Jim was sitting in front of her. She began describing the qualities that attracted her to him – his compassion, his sense of humour, his generosity, his public speaking abilities and his sensuality.

I asked her to focus on these qualities and to draw a symbol representing each one. She drew an ear, a happy face, a mouth and open hands.

Then she proceeded to tell Jim to give her back the compassion that she had loaned him and that he had made his own. She stood up and placed the drawing of the ear on her heart and sat down again.

Next, I calmly invited her to reclaim this compassion and

to make room for it inside her. Judging by how her face lit up and how her body relaxed, I knew that the process was having positive results. Her claiming of the other qualities had the same beneficial effects. She left my office looking radiant and feeling energized.

During the following week, Jim broke his promise never to be alone with her. He invited her to meet him privately. Janet was shaken by Jim's insistence, but was able to tell him that although she still loved him, it was now different. She did not need him in the same way. She said goodbye and left.

The fruits of your loss

Suffering is meaningless unless you claim your legacy.

Losing you revealed
my needs,
my expectations,
my shortcomings,
my dependence.
I did not think I could live without you.

Now that you are gone,
I feel alone and complete at the same time.
I have learned to like the music you loved.
I find myself admiring that which you admired.
I have discovered your areas of interest.
I have started to cook.
I am trying many new things.

I realized that I could help myself, care for myself,
support myself.
I no longer need you to make me feel important.
I am no longer your better half. I am whole.

The strengths I admired in you, I found in myself.
They were there, in need of nourishment
and of room to grow.

In your absence, a miracle is occurring inside me.
The valleys of my soul are being filled,
the riverbeds flow with gushing waters.

I am discovering new sources of energy.
I am enriched by my love for you.

SEPARATION/DIVORCE

After reconciling with yourself, will you be able to reconcile with the other person?

Reconciling with yourself is the most important step. Reconciling with the other person is a sign of complete recovery.

John and Helen are separated but still appreciate getting together to talk about their children.

Paul and Louise spend an evening together occasionally to discuss the many things they still have in common.

Jack always consults his ex-wife on matters regarding his budget.

I feel that a reconciliation is possible if three conditions are met:

1. You must be completely detached emotionally from the other person; otherwise there is a risk of falling back into the old patterns of the relationship.

2. Both of you must have healed your own wounds.

3. Both of you must have matured and become emotionally autonomous.

Very few couples can transform a once hurtful relationship into a fruitful friendship.

You will be filled with a new presence

If you are still looking for the one you lost in your life, if you wish you could see her again, if you are saddened by the mere thought of him, you have not yet let go completely.

If your grieving process is not over yet, know that one day you will be filled with a new and life-giving presence. You will recognize it by the joy, peace and freedom it gives you.

This awakening for women often feels like giving birth. Men feel as if an enormous weight has been lifted from their shoulders.

Your memory will recall the presence of the one you lost; but your love for this person will give this presence new life.

You will no longer be consumed with just physical longing, but by the love you felt for that person. The beloved will no longer be outside of you but living within you in a spiritual way.

All the energy of your love will return to you when you let your beloved go completely.

You are gone now!

This was written by a young woman whose husband died, but it can speak to any significant loss.

You are gone now!
Even though you promised, with or without words,
that you would always love me,
that you would always be by my side,
that you would always be there when I needed you,
that you would always share my joys and my
sorrows.

You are gone now!
And though I revealed myself to you,
there are still so many things that I wanted to say,
so many feelings that I wanted to express,
so many plans that I wanted to fulfill.

You are gone now!
Gradually, I let you go.
I forgive you for leaving so soon, I forget our dreams,
I recover my energy, I ask you to forgive me.

You are gone now!
I know that someday I will stop dying with you,
that the memory of you will be as light and as fragile
as a smile, that a new presence will fill me up,
that all that I loved in you will live inside me.
Then I will be reborn through you.

Saying goodbye: A mother's breakthrough

During a group session, a woman who had lost her baby was able to say goodbye to her child.

A week later, she woke up in the night and experienced an important transformation. She felt very comfortable compared to the many times that she had woken up at night filled with anxiety. Here is what she described:

"I could see pins piercing my heart but I felt no pain.
I understood that I had forgiven myself.
I was able to pray that night.
I was filled with the presence of God, like on the day of my
first communion.

This experience enriched me.
I felt beautiful.
Like someone giving birth.
I felt forever transformed."

Congratulations!

You have survived.
You have learned how to go on living.
You know how to love.

You know how to let go.
You know how to heal.
You know how to grow.

You know how to live.

Because I have known you

Because I have known you, I am not the same.

Thank you for
the love,
the care,
the support,
the gifts,
the romantic dinners,
the exchanges,
the hopes,
the plans,
your intelligence.

Thank you for the loss,
for the opportunity to grow.
I congratulate myself for
questioning my life,
reflecting on myself,
examining my way of loving,
discovering my inner strengths,
exploring the value of suffering,
making new friends and rediscovering old ones,
becoming more sensitive,
expanding my capacity to love,
completing my grieving process.

Also by John Monbourquette

How to Befriend Your Shadow
Welcoming Your Unloved Side

Each of us has a "shadow," composed of everything we have driven back into our unconscious for fear of being rejected by the people we loved when we were young. Over the years, we created a whole underground world filled with things that were shameful, displeasing or upsetting to those around us.

Our task as adults is to rediscover what makes up our shadow, to bring it into the light, and to use it for our own spiritual growth. If we refuse to do this work, we risk being out of balance psychologically, and our lives and relationships will not reach their fullest potential.

Is your shadow your friend or your enemy? That will depend on how you see it and how you relate to it. This book offers you the tools you need to welcome your shadow side. Befriend your shadow, and watch your relationship with yourself and with others grow and deepen!

• 160 pages
• paperback

Also by John Monbourquette

How to Forgive
A Step-by-Step Guide

"What does it take to forgive?" asks John Monbourquette, best-selling author, psychologist and priest. His answer is a unique twelve-step guide that offers profound and practical advice on overcoming the emotional, spiritual and psychological blocks to true forgiveness.

Monbourquette begins by exploring the nature of forgiveness and exploding some of the myths. He shows how essential forgiveness is for us all, whatever our beliefs, for forgiveness touches on all aspects of the human person, the biological and psychological as well as the spiritual. He then takes the reader through his twelve-step healing process, providing practical exercises, case histories, anecdotes and even poetry along the way.

How to Forgive is an honest and touching book that unlocks the liberating and transformative power of forgiveness.

• 198 pages
• paperback

Also by John Monbourquette

How to Discover Your Personal Mission
The Search for Meaning

What is your personal mission in life? Many of us find it hard to answer this question. It is so easy to get caught up in the day-to-day concerns of paying the bills and putting food on the table that we lose sight of the bigger picture. Whether we are young or not so young, we may feel that we haven't quite found our mission, that we're not doing what we feel we should be doing.

How to Discover Your Personal Mission invites you on an adventure to discover your personal mission. In this user-friendly book, best-selling author John Monbourquette leads you through a three-stage process: learning to let go of the past; deepening your sense of identity and mission; and risking a new beginning in life. Through exercises and reflection, you will find the path that leads you in the direction that your soul is calling you. It may appear in the form of an ideal to pursue, a passion, a goal to strive for, or a deep and persistent desire.

Let the journey begin…

- 160 pages
- paperback